The First Steps to Becoming a Real Estate Agent

THE FIRST STEPS TO BECOMING A REAL ESTATE AGENT

An Insight to the Initial Costs of a Career in Real Estate

Henry D. "Hank" Myers

iUniverse, Inc.

New York   Bloomington

The First Steps to Becoming a Real Estate Agent
An Insight to the Initial Costs of a Career in Real Estate

iUniverse books may be ordered through booksellers or by contacting:

iUniverse
1663 Liberty Drive
Bloomington, IN 47403
www.iuniverse.com
1-800-Authors (1-800-288-4677)

Because of the dynamic nature of the Internet, any Web addresses or links contained in this book may have changed since publication and may no longer be valid.

The views expressed in this work are solely those of the author and do not necessarily reflect the views of the publisher, and the publisher hereby disclaims any responsibility for them.

ISBN: 978-0-595-48929-9 (pbk)
ISBN: 978-0-595-60898-0 (ebk)

Printed in the United States of America

Contents

Acknowledgments

Most of us never get to stand on a stage as grand or as widely viewed as the one reserved for presentation of the Oscars. Nor do we have the opportunity to thank those in our own lives, as the actors and actresses do while on that stage. But most of us are blessed with just as many helpful people in our own lives. They are the people whom we never publicly get to acknowledge as instrumental in the successes in our lives, however insignificant those successes—and our lives—may seem to us.

We usually have our immediate family on whose support we can often always rely. To choose any particular family member to acknowledge solely, in my case, is very difficult. I am the youngest of seven children, and we often paired in groups of two or three when we played together as children. This pairing was usually done according to the nearness in age. Despite the groupings according to age association, we have always been inseparable and even clannish in our defense of each other regardless of the age differences.

My sister just two years my elder is by nature petite and delicate, and was often neither interested nor allowed to engage in the activities of our older and more physically capable siblings. Therefore, she was usually stuck with only me as a playmate. For as long as I remember she has been there for me and has always been very understanding of her younger brother's vulnerability and shortcomings. In our mature lives, she has remained a priceless friend and supporter of my wildest dreams and ideas. To express my appreciation for her continued support these many, many years, I will simply say, "Thank you, Geri."

As we wander through life's roads—those taken and not taken—we are fortunate to bump into people outside our biological family who, for whatever reasons, become friends. Twenty-five years ago, I found such a friend in Richard Roza. Rich has always been patient, often to the point of his own frustration, with my ranting over situations in my real estate career as well as the normal ups and downs in my life outside my career. He has been the best and least criticizing "ear" not attached to my own head that I could hope for. Loyal, honest, and steadfast, he is a true friend. For always listening to me, supporting my crazy whims, and being my friend, "Thank you, Rich."

Sometimes we find co-workers who occasionally, in their special way, stand out among the rest. Marcia Wallace Chittenden is one of those for me. She has dragged me, screaming and kicking, toward becoming more technologically capable. We completed our first paperless transaction together, at her persistence, in 2006. Though twelve years my senior, she has more energy and enthusiasm than I could ever hope for. She planted the seed in my head, then nudged me forward to write this book. "Thank you, Marcia."

Introduction

So, you think you want to become a Real Estate Agent? Please allow me to speak candidly to help you "think" about that idea.

I have always tried to help the underdog whenever I thought I had any positive concepts or energy to share. Some may consider that a personal weakness, but my birthright is rooted in the Ozarks of Southern Missouri as the son of a tenant farmer. The soil there was so poor "you couldn't raise a good fight on it." All the folks in that area were pretty much in the same situation and were always eager to offer a helping hand. That characteristic of helpfulness, if not bred into me, was easily acquired at a very early age and accepted as the decent thing to do when a need was recognized.

Hopefully, what I have to say will be a help rather than a negative influence on you, who have had the nagging thought in the back of your head, or the sudden inspiration, to "become a Real Estate Agent."

Many unsuspecting souls think that being a realty agent is an easy, get-rich-quick job that requires no special skills and even less hard work. I have been a REALTOR® * for twenty years, and learned the profession by using a lot of effort, common sense, and by completing many continuing education courses. I know that most people don't have the foggiest idea of what it takes to be a successful agent. Most people have even less of an idea of how expensive it can be just to obtain a license and join the necessary organizations to get started.

This writing is not designed to help new agents become successful. It is to share with new and prospective agents some of the pitfalls in thinking that becoming a successful realty agent can be accomplished without any time-consuming effort, that once they are licensed they are immediately and inalienably guaranteed success, and that money will just roll into their pocket because they are permitted to sell real estate.

If my offering helps anyone become successful, I will have given that person a gift. He or she may take it and use it freely.

My experience as a Real Estate Agent has been in California only, and I recognize that the laws in other states differ widely. California has been a consistent leader in setting standards of practice in real estate and is often on the cutting edge of incorporating practices that are required to complete real estate transactions.

The reason for this is very simple. California is one of the most litigious states in our country, especially concerning the transference of real estate. It is said that one out of every six real estate transactions ends up in litigation.

I will say right here and now that I am not an attorney of any kind, nor am I a certified public accountant. Make a great big note right here. My disclosure of those two facts sits at the heart of all real estate practice. "Disclose, disclose, disclose!"

I know that a multitude of people out there are just waiting to rip this culmination of words to shreds. This writing is not intended to meet anyone's preconceived notion of what should be given to the public concerning the real estate industry.

My purpose here is solely to broach the subject of costs to the novice who is "thinking" about becoming, or has just recently received the license to become, a real estate professional.

The real estate marketplace is vulnerable to cycles, just like any other industry. When the housing market is enjoying the ascending cycle, many people who want to make a few fast bucks think they can jump in on the good times and become rich overnight. This is especially true of those who have maintained their license but have been inactive since the end of the last ascending cycle.

There are also those who may be recently retired, or those who think they can be a successful realty agent by working in real estate as a second job or just on weekends. There was a time when this could have been a reality. Many successful agents started their careers when that mindset worked.

Today, a real estate career is not the most user-friendly pursuit for Mr. Mom, the Soccer Mom, or anyone else who wants a part-time job. The real estate industry has become far too technical and is pockmarked with so many legal issues that a minefield may look like a cake walk by comparison.

When the cycle moves from boom to bust, as it always does, many of those agents who get into the business during the "upside" of the cycle soon realize that surviving the "downside" of the cycle is impossible. They quickly return to the safer and more reliable "nine to five" that pays the bills and gives some sense of regularity and sanity. Those who do survive the downside do so by plying great resolve, fortitude, and every possible skill they can master.

Most beginners are not even aware of the costs that have to be paid before they finally become nothing more than another big disappointment in the junkyard of discarded real estate careers. The costs are not just financial but also emotional, and they are sometimes devastating to what was once a loving family relationship.

As stated above, this is not a primer to teach anyone to become successful as a real estate agent or to make a fortune by investing in real estate. There is already enough written to guide those individuals. This offering is a blunt, if not brutal, insight into the basic costs of embarking on the journey as a career real estate agent.

If you are seriously considering becoming a real estate agent, do not allow me to discourage you, but you need to clearly focus on the costs. Do not try to hide them deeply in the small print of a real estate primer that approaches the volume of *War and Peace*. They will not magically disappear.

On the personal level, a career in real estate is not a fantasy. It is a real profession with realities that can be as fatal in monetary and emotional costs as any war.

So, "Go not blindly into the den of lions."

*REALTOR® is a federally registered collective membership mark which identifies a real estate professional who is a Member of the NATIONAL ASSOCIATION OF REALTORS® and subscribes to its strict Code of Ethics.

Author's Note: Use of the word Realtor(s)® on the back cover and in part of the text is used for educational purposes to illustrate to the public and prospective real estate agents the "permitted (but not preferred)" use of the MARKS which belong to the NATIONAL ASSOCIATION OF REALTORS®. The preferred use would be REALTOR®.

Chapter 1

▼

The Fallacy

"I get my license, join a brokerage, get to set my own work schedule, make sales quickly and easily, and receive large commission checks without breaking a sweat."

Let's carefully look at that concept; otherwise, we may very well end up derailed before we even get the engine started.

Sure, you can purchase the home study courses or take the minimal number of required courses at the local junior college for a few hundred bucks. If you are lucky and pass the licensing exam on the first try, congratulations—you're an excellent student. However, very little of what you learn in order to pass the test is useful in the day-to-day work as an agent.

I earned a Bachelor of Science degree by working my way through college, and I had begun work on my master's degree before winning the "military lottery" in 1969. For those who remember, that lottery was not necessarily one you wanted to win.

I knew how to study and was not your average idiot, yet it took five attempts before I passed the 250-question, three-hour exam to become licensed. Having grown up on farms in the Midwest, I already knew how many square feet there are in an acre of land, and I knew how to tell in which direction the sun rises and sets, and where north and south are. But believe me when I tell you, understanding the thinking process of those who design the California real estate licensing exam really does force you to think beyond your normal framework of logic.

After you have spent your first "few hundred bucks" and at least six weeks of time for your education, you may pass the exam on the first shot. Know that rarely can you take the licensing exam the day after you qualify to do so. You must schedule the exam and usually travel a good distance to one of the exam sites. Waiting for an exam date may cost you another couple of months.

Now, with new license in hand, you must decide, "With which broker do I wish to work?"

> New licensees should not expect to complete a transaction for at least three months after they become licensed.
>
> ***This is just the first cold, hard fact.***

Most brokers start new licensees on a brokerage split of 50 percent. Let's take a typical bread-and-butter transaction in most of the well-populated cities in California as an example. Most three-bedroom, one-or two-bath, 1,000-to 1,500-square-foot ranch-style homes built any date from 1950 through 1980 will sell for $500,000.

Be aware that the price may vary slightly depending on whether it is a buyer's market or a seller's market and what decade you read this example. "Prices are subject to change without notice." Where have we heard that disclaimer—and how often?

If you are lucky, you may obtain a listing and negotiate a commission of 6 percent of the sales price; or, if you represent buyers, the home they want to buy will be listed with a 6 percent commission.

Understand that commissions are not set by law. They are negotiated between the agent and seller. Commissions may range from 1 percent to 10 percent depending on the circumstances, property, and negotiating skills of both the agent and the seller.

Typically, your broker will receive half of a commission and another broker will receive the other half. It is not the norm for an agent to list a property and also find the buyer for that listing. So, with a 6 percent commission on a $500,000 property, your broker (usually) will receive $15,000 as the gross commission.

Most brokers must take 6 percent of the gross commission right off the top to pay for the Corporate Franchise Fee. Brokerages are often "independently owned" but may be affiliated or franchised with one of the "Big Five" nationwide brokerage firms. This top 6 percent of the gross commission goes toward paying for that affiliation.

So now the $15,000 has just been reduced to $14,100, from which the broker gives you your 50 percent split, and you receive $7,050.

With your paycheck in hand, you feel "Saturday-night rich." You should go to the mall and "shop 'til you drop," right?

Wrong!

You are an Independent Contractor and you pay your own taxes. Your broker does not pay them for you.

This is the second cold, hard fact.

You must remember your Rich Uncle. You need to plan to pay taxes on your windfall. To be safe, you probably should figure the IRS will get 25 percent of your gross earnings. You will have to pay an estimated tax each quarter of the year, and your gross earnings will ultimately determine what your tax bracket will be. But for the sake of our example, your net windfall becomes $5,287.50.

Another "Uncle" you will need to plan to contribute to is your local municipality. Once you are discovered as a person who is conducting business and making money in the town or city where you ply your trade, you will have to pay for a license to do so.

This may be a flat fee or it may be based on your gross earnings for the year, and it is usually due at the end of the local municipality's fiscal year. This may cost you anywhere from $50 to $500 on average. If you routinely sell real estate in more than one municipality, you may have to have a license in each of those communities, not just in the one where your public business office is located.

Depending on the marketplace and your skill as an agent, you may not close your second transaction for several months. A safe rule of thumb is to budget at least six months in advance for all of your living expenses. Living can become very uncomfortable if you are down to your last $100 and you don't have anything in escrow.

Keep in mind that if you are not in escrow, you are not employed. You only have a license to sell real estate. Oh, yeah—your state issued license has also cost you a couple of hundred dollars.

"What?"

Once you pass the exam, do you think the state just *gives* you the license?

Are we approaching the truth about the instant fortune to be made as a real estate agent? Read on Mc Duff.

CHAPTER 2

▼

HIDDEN COSTS

Oh! Did I forget to mention that before you get to the end of the first sale, you will need to cover a few up-front costs before you can even start to work with most brokerages?

Before you can actively and freely work with most brokerages, you will need to join your local Multiple Listing Service (MLS). The MLS is the organization through which all cooperating brokers may share their listings in return for a shared (usually equally) commission earned on each listing. The MLS is the tool you need to give your listings maximum local exposure to all other agents who are also members. The MLS greatly increases your chances that another agent will bring a buyer to your listings. Unless there is an extremely compelling reason, all sellers should insist on their property being listed in the local MLS. The widest exposure and best chance for obtaining the highest price for their property is gained when it is listed in the MLS.

National data bases access local MLSs to create their websites and are viewed from anywhere in the world via the Internet. Remember: it is a very small percentage of listings that are sold by the listing agent himself or herself.

Joining the local MLS will cost you perhaps $1,000. There are annual expenses of another couple of hundred dollars, either annually or biannually, to continue being a member of your MLS.

You will also want or need to belong to your Local Association of Realtors®. This will also cost you a couple of hundred dollars annually. Your local membership may or may not include some of the cost of belonging to the National Association of Realtors® and any State Association of Realtors® where you live.

To access listed properties, key safes are usually installed on your and other agent's listings. You will need a key safe for each of your listings. You will also need a key card to access all the key safes on listings you want to see that belong to other agents. A key card will cost a couple of hundred dollars, and each key safe will cost another hundred or so. You will probably want six key safes for your potential listings. The electronic key card is usually leased from the company that makes the card. Renewal of the lease—yes, I said *lease*—will cost another couple of hundred dollars each year.

Now we get to signs for use on your listings. Typical 18" by 24" plasticized corrugated cardboard signs run about $25 each. These are the least expensive descent size signs to purchase. Signs with your picture on them will cost more, but basic signs with just your name and phone numbers are the cheapest way to get started.

If you are lucky, your broker will be so happy to have you join his or her firm that he will spring for the first five or six generic company signs and hardware (posts) to help you get into business. You will, however, be required to pay for your replacements as you need them. Strong winds and graffiti artists can easily destroy a half-dozen signs within a normal three-to six-month listing period.

You will also need at least four Open House signs to direct traffic to your open house events. These will cost you from $25 to $30 each. If you breach local ordinances with the placement of these signs, they may be confiscated by local authorities during your open house event. They may also be stolen by vandals just for fun. Flags are also great collectables for vandals and children. Flags will cost you about $15 each.

Any riders for your signs will cost extra, and you will have to spring for those on your own. But these cost only about $10 to $15 per rider, and you probably won't need more than a half-dozen to get started.

Many brokers will also give you your first 500 or maybe 1,000 business cards, which will cost you, on average, $65 per 1,000 to replace. You can easily use 1,000 business cards per month if you are diligent in "farming" and passing out cards to the public in order to become a household name. You will also drop a card every time you preview a property during broker caravan (see below) and when showing properties to customers.

Errors and omissions insurance will be required on each transaction. This may be available to you for about $200 per transaction, or your broker may require you to pay it in advance each year with his or her policy, or the corporate policy if applicable. Annual fees for E&O are typically $1,500 to $2,000 per agent if paid up front.

Oh, you didn't expect *these* costs?

Don't forget the additional insurance for your vehicle. You will be carrying people in your car for business purposes, and you will need to cover them in case you have an accident. If you ever have an accident with clients/customers in your vehicle, you will be glad you have the additional coverage. In addition, your broker will require that his company is also named on your policy. Allow another $500 each year for this cost.

You may have to run your own ads for your open houses, and you may need additional advertising to placate some of your more demanding sellers. You may also want or need to advertise in any number of "glossy" magazines for additional exposure, especially for some of your more discriminating listings. These ads aren't cheap. A "glossy" can cost up to $800 or more per month for a single listing.

Are we making money yet?

If you have a listing that is receiving fewer than multiple offers once it hits the MLS, you may have to sit open house on it every Sunday, or at least every other Sunday, to make it available to potential buyers until it is sold. Most sellers will expect open houses on Sunday afternoons.

Get used to this idea. You may actually have to work a little bit.

During the down cycle of the real estate market, you may have a listing for as long as a year before it is sold. When you hold open house, you may wish to serve some small refreshments to maintain the appearance of graciousness and hospitality. There is a cost for refreshments. You will pay for this, not your broker.

Not getting any cooperation or showings from your fellow agents?

Broker open caravan, or broker's tour, is usually held once each week through most MLSs and is designed for all agents to preview new listings that have come on the market during the week. Broker caravan refers to agents or groups of agents who may carpool to view properties that are listed on broker's tour. Broker's tour includes listings that may have previously been available for agents to see by appointment only.

Typically, you can sponsor a broker open on the same property at least once each month. If there are a large number of houses on the broker's tour each week, be prepared to offer refreshments and even free gifts for a drawing as enticement to attract agents to your listing.

The gift for a drawing can be a $25 or $50 gift card from any store or gas station. Lotto tickets are also popular enticements. Real estate agents are prone to playing the odds. If you need an example of the odds, consider the chances of obtaining a listing, opening a transaction, and then successfully closing it.

To illustrate these odds, let's take the current descending market in the city where I work, which has approximately 200,000 residents. During the month of July, 2007 there were approximately 1,200 active listings in our MLS. There were approximately 3,500 active agents who consummated approximately only five purchase agreements each day.

Using these raw numbers, only an average of 34 percent of the agents had a listing. Keep in mind that by averaging, the true story is lost. Those who have a listing, typically have more than one.

At the above rate of sales per day with two agents being involved in each sale, it would take 120 days for each agent in our MLS to complete one sale. The fact is that not every agent had a listing or a buyer for one of the 1,200 listings.

In the unreal occurrence that each agent would be involved in only one transaction until the entire inventory is depleted (without any listings being added) during the 120 days, it is easy to see how great the odds are that each agent would successfully complete a sale during that time frame.

When an offer is accepted, there are more than 100 items to be disclosed on each property sold in California during the transaction. Any one disclosure may result in the buyer rejecting the property and there is usually a loan that must receive final approval before the sale can be completed. Plus, all items of concern that are discovered by any inspection performed by the buyer must be addressed and negotiated to the satisfaction of both the buyer and seller before the transaction can proceed to it's successful completion.

This is precisely what I mean by realty agents being prone to playing the odds. Perhaps I should restate this by saying "Real estate agents are an extremely optimistic group of people."

Agents burn a lot of gas each week while previewing properties and showing potential buyers properties they (agents) have seen on broker open caravan/tours. Most agents appreciate the odds of winning a $50 gas card or winning the lotto (so they can retire) just for seeing a property on the weekly broker's tour.

You need to do the math!

If your new career appears to be the proverbial "money pit," it is all money well spent, but it does run up the tab for being a real estate agent. You may try to beat the system by cutting corners on these costs, but you will reap only what you sow.

Investing in just the basics outlined here will save you time in the end, and you will come to understand acutely the meaning of the phrase "Time is money."

You will eventually learn to waste neither.

Chapter 3

▼

The Internet—Your Indispensable Home Tool Chest

Don't underestimate the power of the Internet in real estate today. The media say that in the mid-1990s less than 5 percent of the public used the Internet to search for property and an agent to help them buy or sell a property. Today over 80 percent of all real estate searches by buyers and sellers are initiated on the Internet.

You will need a home office with Internet capability in order to "be on top" of your business as an agent. If you get a call from a potential client (seller) or customer (buyer) at 9:00 p.m. on either your cell phone or residential phone, you will probably need to have the MLS database at your command when you talk to them. Therefore, you will want at least the basic office equipment at your fingertips, because when a client/customer calls, she will be listening very carefully to see if you are the agent with whom she truly wishes to work. Being Internet and computer savvy is the initial litmus test.

She will expect you to immediately give her answers concerning all properties in your area that are of interest to her. It may be impossible for you to know what new listing came on the market that she has just now seen pop up on her computer screen. You will need to access the MLS database immediately to be in sync with her inquiry.

If you don't have a computer, a Blackberry, or a Palm Pilot to accesses your MLS, you probably will not have the opportunity to speak with that potential client/customer again. Customers want instant gratification and already know almost as much about your market inventory as you do, because they have been studying the market on the Internet for at least several weeks before they select the agent with whom they think they can be comfortable enough to make contact. You will either win or lose a customer/client within the first couple of minutes of the initial phone conversation.

It may seem rather presumptuous for them to have worked for several weeks privately and then, the first time they call you, expect up-to-the-minute details about a property you may not even know exists. It is not presumptuous. Knowing the entire inventory all the time is crucial in the real estate business. If you don't know the inventory, how can you possibly expect to sell it?

A website is a must for capturing clients and customers. Internet searches for property and agents are quickly outpacing printed information, because news in print is no longer "news" but rather "instant history." Newspaper companies are feeling the heat from the Internet and are beginning to sweat!

Personal websites can be pricey depending on how sophisticated you wish to be perceived. The cost of websites is a whole other issue that requires more time and space than I have allotted here. Websites vary greatly in content and features. They will vary in price accordingly. Good ballpark figures can range from $100 to$400 per month.

Public access to your local MLS is a plus and a minus—a real dou-ble-edged sword. You may not be required to schlep potential buyers all over town searching for the right property out of the five or ten that you would have selected for them to see. They usually have already screened most of the properties that are available and will have likely narrowed down the properties they wish to visit to two or three. This will save you time and gas money, unless you lose them by not being "on the same page" as they are in regard to immediate MLS access the first time they call.

You will need a good computer and a high-speed Internet connection to download the large amount of data that is available in your MLS, and do it quickly. A good system will cost about $1,500 plus your Internet Service Provider (ISP) connection of approximately $50 per month, and a dedicated line for another $5 per month.

You will probably find it necessary to have a laptop with printer capa-bility in order to conduct business from your vehicle, in a restaurant, in a hotel, or in their home when an appointment in your office is not readily possible. This is easily another $1,500, not counting the cost for remote accessibility for your laptop.

Most agents prefer to have a fax/copier/scanner/printer in their home office too. If you have to keep running to your public business office at all hours of the day (your stolen day off) and night to fax a piece of paper to a client, you will waste a lot of time. Plus, it is very inconvenient at 9:00 p.m. when you are already in your pajamas.

If you have the basic equipment at your home, your clients/customers will recognize that you are on top of your business. They will appreciate working with you and more likely perceive you as being "professional." You will also need a dedicated fax line. Hanging up the phone to use your fax can be very awkward and you will not appear seamless as a professional. An all-in-one piece of equipment will cost about $400, and a dedicated line may cost as little as $5 per month.

Clients and customers expect immediate service and access to their agent now more than ever before. Needless to say, a cell phone is a must. Figure at least $200 for the phone and equipment and $40 per month for just the most basic connection and usage minutes.

You will also probably prefer to take your own pictures of your listings. You will need a digital camera so you can quickly upload pictures to your computer and then to your local MLS and your website. You can hire this done or perhaps your brokerage will do it for you for a cost, but it is quicker and you have more control over the product if you do it yourself. You will also save a lot of time by posting your listing in the MLS immediately instead of waiting several days for someone else to do it. A digital camera and equipment with this capability will cost another two to three hundred dollars.

Brace yourself!

I will venture to say that by 2015, it will probably become necessary to offer electronic signatures to clients who travel often and who wish to purchase their properties using their laptop during business trips. Or those who are using their PC at home when they are moving to your area from out of state and need to sign the documents required in their transaction.

When the transaction is complete, you will burn it to a CD and give them the entire transaction on a CD rather than have them collect a paper file that is three to four inches thick.

This technology is now available and will probably be the preferred real estate technology within the next five to ten years. I was involved with my first paperless transaction in 2006. Believe me when I tell you that as the majority of agents catch on to this technology, it will definitely be the technology of choice for home sales and purchases.

Subscription to the paperless transaction capability (RELAY®) and electronic signatures (DocuSign™) will easily add another $100 per month to your expense tab. But it will pay for itself in time and paper saved—not to mention the storage space and/or cost to keep your files for the legally required five years after the transaction has been completed.

Being a real estate agent requires these basic financial costs just to perform the functions of sharing and exchanging information in the real estate industry. At this point, you may view your new career not just as a money pit, but a bottomless money pit.

You must plan on these costs and treat your career like a business. It is not just a job. It is a career that requires a commitment. If you think of your business as "the job you are currently involved in or working," you will not be successful, nor will you last as a real estate agent. You will end up wasting a lot of your time, energy, and money. Plus, you may very well get sued during the process.

If you ever lose a lawsuit you may destroy your financial security for many years to come.

This is the third cold hard fact.

It is very important to understand the difference between being involved and being committed. The best example of this is a ham and egg breakfast. The chicken that laid the egg was involved … the pig was committed.

Don't forget that.

CHAPTER 4

▼

THE COST OF PERSONAL TIME AND STRESS

As stated earlier, time is money. Any respectable book that speaks of careers in real estate will usually slip you the hint that you may end up working sixty to eighty hours per week. That may well be true, depending on your commitments and the volume of business you are handling at any particular time. Even if you aren't working sixty or more hours every week, there will be those weeks that you will. Sometimes you may work those kinds of hours for a few months at a time. These are obligations and responsibilities real estate agents learn to embrace.

During those times, you will need to focus on what is on your plate until you can shove back from the table and call it a meal. The dining may be worth it, but the downside is that you can carry a heavy load as a result of the feast. The "load" refers to the strain on your own nerves and the stress your family or significant other may also experience.

What price do you put on missing the Super Bowl game because that is the only time your client or customer is able to meet with you to sign disclosure documents? Or perhaps that is the only time you can finally write the contract for the customer who has been trying to make the final choice between two properties for the past three days?

What is the cost when you must meet work commitments instead of attending your child's baseball or soccer games for three weeks in a row? Evenings and weekends are prime times to conduct real estate business, because that is often the only, or at least most convenient, time your clients are available to you.

The attempt to balance work-related demands and the demands of personal relationships often fails. Unless you have a finely tuned ability to effectively manage tight schedules and intense emotions, all parties may suffer. There are exceptions, but difficult schedules appear to have become the norm in the United States during the last half of the twentieth century.

Realty agents need to be accessible to customers and clients every day of the week, and often 24/7 (or at least from 6:00 a.m. until 8:00 p.m. or 9:00 p.m.). It is not uncommon for an agent to be actively working five or more clients/customers at any given time. Those clients'/customers' schedules do not always work well within the agent's personal schedule. Stress on the agent can easily reach the maximum level when a family with children is involved.

One customer with whom I worked would often call me only after 11:00 p.m. It was a high priced sale that we were working on, but I also paid a high price for being available at that hour for three months until the correct home was found and the transaction closed. She was ultimately happy with the purchase and with my service to her.

If you do not handle "totally upset apple carts" very well, you may not need to look beyond this point at a career in real estate. Some transactions progress very smoothly from beginning to end, but some just seem to be trouble from day one. Experience and skill often mitigate any disaster when all parties are truly working for a good and common goal. There are many cases when all the hard work and best intentions of all parties still will not save a transaction.

I recently reached the point in a transaction where loan documents had been issued to escrow. At 4:30 p.m. the afternoon before the buyer was scheduled to sign the documents (at 8:00 a.m. the following morning), the lender notified escrow to not allow the documents to be signed because the lender had just filed bankruptcy. This happened just days before the escrow was to close.

It happened after a nine-month marketing period and a twice-extended escrow period. It was like having only one nerve left and someone had started to tap dance on it while wearing a pair of track shoes that were out-fitted with double cleats.

The buyer had a very capable loan broker who saved the transaction with her fast thinking and her ability to apply for a new loan quickly with two other lenders. The escrow closed within ten days. However, many loan brokers aren't as sharp, committed, or on top of their work as she was.

Everyone's nerves were frayed during the last ten days of that escrow, but all of us were on the same page and worked hard for the common goal. Nobody "lost it."

If you are tender of heart or find it hard to accept unexpected blows below the belt, then perhaps the real estate fight is not your best choice of sport.

Many years ago, I received an innocent enough request from a buyer's agent asking that the seller (whom I represented) would allow the buyers to "paint" the interior of the vacant house the weekend before the escrow was supposed to close. It was scheduled to close the following Tuesday. The seller agreed to allow the buyers access to paint, and the buyers were given a key that Friday afternoon. I checked the property the following Monday morning only to discover that an entire wall had been removed and all the sheetrock had been removed from several other walls as well as from most of the ceilings throughout the house. The buyer's intent was to remodel the entire house, not just paint.

The closing was delayed until the following Friday because of a financing glitch. Fortunately, the escrow did close. But until it did, the stress level was unimaginable, and focusing on anything else that week was virtually impossible.

I still have those pictures to remind me to **never give up a key until the escrow closes.**

The number of similar war stories I have heard would fill volumes, and most are humorous … at a distance. But when it is up close and personal it is a totally different story, and it may require several days to recover from such a trauma. The cost in stress from that one was far more expensive than the money earned in commission. That lesson was very expensive emotionally and will never be forgotten.

Stress from personality differences between buyers, sellers, and agents can also reach a crescendo that would rival Shostakovich's "Festive Overture" and Tchaikovsky's "1812 Overture"—combined.

When similar events happen, as they sometimes will, those with less than brave hearts and strong emotion-control skills may find that the cost to personal relationships, especially in families, is incalculable. Personal relationships often do not survive these kinds of events when they come frequently or in rapid succession. Unfortunately, not everyone can easily adjust to these kinds of demands.

> It is not uncommon for personal relationships and marriages to fall victim to the stress of real estate careers and many end up shattered or in divorce.
>
> *This is the fourth cold hard fact.*

When this happens to anyone, life can become just the plain old "pits."

The costs in personal time and emotion have a very high price tag. Prospective real estate agents should carefully consider these kinds of unexpected events before making the commitment to a career in real estate.

If this is not your cup of tea, don't even attempt to drink it. It can be very bitter.

CHAPTER 5

▼

THE COST OF "HELPFUL" CO-WORKERS

The novice in his first office can often be given truly helpful advice and direction from honest and respectful agents. There are some agents, however, who cannot seem to forego their finely honed and sometimes innate skill to control everyone they meet.

The novice may be given a lead to a potential client or customer by an agent who is looking to make a fast and easy buck on the backs of new agents. Many "up calls" that come into an office from a sign or an ad may be "given" to a new agent by an agent who does not want to work with that particular client/customer. Perhaps the "up" is inquiring about a property that is located in an area of town or a neighborhood with which the original receiving agent is not familiar. Or maybe that agent simply refuses to work the particular neighborhood or type of property the caller is inquiring about. In order to capture the caller's business for the office, the original receiving agent will offer the lead to the novice—for a fee.

Industry-wide, referral fees from one agent to another are typically 25 percent of the gross commission. That's a pretty nice piece of pocket change for simply turning over a call to someone else.

I, being the "nice guy" that I am, had this happen to me for years until I finally realized I could negotiate referral fees with agents in my own office. I don't know how many "referrals" I received this way until I finally caught on to what was really happening. I thought the others agents were trying to be nice to me and even help me obtain more business.

What some of those agents really wanted was simply an easy buck from someone else who would literally do all the work. And the potential sale was one on which the referring agent would not spend his time, effort, or money anyway.

Figure the cost of referrals in time and money. If you are new and working on a 50 percent broker split, by giving 25 percent for the referral (and doing all the work), you are working for only 25 percent of a commission that is usually going to be based on a lower priced property. If it were an expensively priced property, you could bet that agent would not be referring it to anyone else.

If you have no business this can help you get started, but if you already have some active clients of your own, this additional business may be more costly in terms of your time than it is profitable in terms of actual dollars.

Partnering with other agents can also be a very costly proposition. Partnerships must be very well spelled out, even down to the last detail in regard to the duties and financial investments of each partner. The duties of each agent need to be well defined and the commission split must be fifty-fifty. Otherwise, one of the partners will eventually feel shortchanged and those feelings will probably be legitimate.

If there is an advantage in the partnership, either because it creates more business volume or because it allows agents some time off that they would not normally be able to schedule, the partnership can be a good thing.

Offering two agents for the price of one to the buyer or seller can also be a plus in some ways, but the liability for each partner is doubled.

Both partners will have to communicate very closely, and both will have to know exactly what the other is doing at all times. If your partner says something or does something that results in a law suit, you will also be sued because you are a partner in the transaction.

Knowing when to retire from a career in real estate seems to be one of the most difficult things for agents to learn. A career in real estate is often viable employment for many agents in their seventies and even into their eighties because it is less a physical activity than it is an intellectual activity.

The standing joke is that "Old real estate agents never die. They just keep listing ... and listing ... and listing, until they finally list over into their graves." That joke may be more truthful than the humor implies.

Many agents want to retire but just can't seem to refuse "one more transaction." This business can become somewhat addictive. When an agent still has his or her mental faculties intact and no debilitating physical limitations, why not earn just one more commission?

Realistically, there comes a time in all careers when the career should end, and end completely.

This is the fifth cold, hard fact.

Agents who wish to retire will often look for a younger agent to "help them retire." What this means is the retiring agent wants to feed leads (usually former clients, or potential clients who have been referred by former clients) to the younger agent and then collect the 25 percent referral fee.

This can be a beneficial arrangement for the younger agent up to a point. But there must be an end to the arrangement. That is only fair to both parties.

The younger agent should not be expected to become the source of a pension for the retiring agent. Without a definite end to the arrangement, the retiring agent may want to retire at seventy-five years of age, then live to be one hundred. If that happens without an expiration date to the agreement, it may have become a twenty-five-year pension plan at the expense of the younger agent.

All of the above arrangements have subtle costs that are usually quite costly to someone. All arrangements regarding co-workers and particularly partnerships must be in writing and have an expiration date, just like listing contracts. Otherwise, they can very quickly become expensive investments with diminishing returns.

CHAPTER 6

▼

TIME SPENT IN NECESSARY MEETINGS AND EVENTS

Time will have to be allotted for necessary meetings scheduled by the broker, meetings with the local association, and seminars.

Agents are Independent Contractors, and unless meetings are mandatory, agents cannot be made to attend. If the broker and local association are worthy and function properly in their roles, agents can receive real benefits that justify paying the broker split and the association dues.

If agents are fortunate, their broker will conduct productive and informative office meetings. Those meetings are typically scheduled each week. The purpose of the meeting should be to help all agents stay abreast of legal issues that keep them and their clients out of court. The meeting should also allow agents to relay information about situations that are occurring in their transactions, which can be helpful in resolving issues other agents may have to face someday.

Office meetings should be an indispensable source for staying up to date on inventory and trends in the local marketplace. They are an excellent opportunity to hobnob, learn, and share experiences with fellow agents in their office.

Local association boards usually have meetings for all members of the board and/or MLS on a monthly or quarterly basis. These can be very helpful and informative. Often there are guest speakers whose expertise can prove invaluable to real estate careers.

These meetings also usually provide information concerning events and/or procedures that affect local organizational rules. MLS rules are designed to help agents conduct business properly within the local association, and without harming other agents or the public at large.

The broker and local association should keep agents informed about seminars that become available either locally or at some distance, and particularly those that may be very helpful to attend.

These seminars usually are beneficial to a real estate career, and agents may be able to receive state Department of Real Estate Continuing Education credits by attending them. On a two-, three-, or four-year basis, most states require license renewal. In order to renew, an agent will need to accumulate a prescribed number of credits.

Any number of these seminars can be very informative, but some may not be much more than an opportunity for the speaker to promote himself and his products. The types of products that are made available through these seminars include CDs, workbooks, and "learning camps." Some are quite helpful, but many are nothing more than promotional and can be very expensive.

Some seminars are free and are sponsored by local boards, industry affiliates, or individual brokers. Many seminars are available to agents that will have to be paid from their own resources. These seminars can range in price from $25 to $2,000 per agent.

New agents will need to attend several of these before they will be able to identify which ones they really want or need to attend in the future. Going to these takes up a good deal of time, energy, and money, but there really is no better way to learn than to just go—until the agent can make a proper decision about the value of each future opportunity.

Most of these meetings are beneficial, but many will not be very productive. If agents end up using these as social events rather than information-gathering opportunities, the agents may need to evaluate their priorities. Prioritizing sits at the very core of balancing an agent's personal and business life.

A good indicator of the value of the meeting may be what is served as refreshments. Agents need to watch out for sugar cookies, donuts, and Danishes that are washed down with bottomless cups of strong coffee. Otherwise, they are liable to become excited beyond reason and mistake genuine enthusiasm for the sugar and caffeine high. The "sugar high" is an old sales manager's tactic to induce pseudo-enthusiasm disguised as genuine motivation.

Without digressing into mendacity, it is worthy to say that it is easy to miss the subtleties of speakers who need a popularity or ego boost. Speakers with this type of agenda are not limited to those in fee seminars.

If office meetings often digress to not much more than corporate touting, or local association meetings frequently become stumps for political influence, an agent needs to strongly evaluate his or her need to participate.

The weekly work schedule must incorporate time for broker open houses/broker tours. The broker tour day will easily consume four to six hours every week. Office meetings will also consume two to three hours each week, allowing for refreshments and materials collected prior to each meeting. Meetings usually are limited to one hour but often run into overtime. By the time agents resume their work activities, they will easily have spent two or three hours. One full day each week can easily be spent on just these two events.

Agents, especially new agents, should be discriminatory in the time they spend in meetings and seminars. Otherwise, they can waste valuable work time and fail to increase their bottom line.

To recapitulate: remember, agents are Independent Contractors, not employees. Agents are solely responsible for determining how valuable their time is and how they need to spend it. Time wasted in non-productive meetings can easily eat up time that could have been spent working, with family, or a favorite recreation.

Balance in an agent's life has a very high value. No dollar amount can be placed on that. Unnecessarily wasted time in meetings and at events is a cost that can never be recovered.

▼

CHAPTER 7

AUXILIARY COSTS

If the costs mentioned in previous chapters are not high enough, the new agent should be on the alert for auxiliary costs during a transaction. Buyers and sellers often discover that benefits and financial shortcomings during a transaction catch them off guard.

When a buyer realizes a home protection plan will not be paid by the seller when one has been requested, or when he is short several hundred dollars to pay certain costs for repairs and the seller refuses to pay for them, he may look to receive those funds from the nearest target. That target is often the agent or agents.

If a seller cannot or will not pay for a home protection plan for the buyer, and needs to replace a few window screens or install GFI outlets to keep the buyer happy, he too may look for assistance to have these or any number of small items covered by the agents.

The onus then rests on the agent's shoulders, or should I say pockets, to find a solution to complete the transaction. Many times the easiest solution is for the agents to pony up and get the deal closed—especially if the cost is minor or does not exceed a couple of hundred dollars. Paying even a penny out of agent's pocket is solely up to the discretion of the agent or agents involved. Of course, the transaction can fall apart if all parties become obstinate.

Proper counseling and discussion of these potential expenses should be thoroughly covered before pen ever reaches paper, otherwise these types of auxiliary costs may become quite costly during the transaction.

Clients and customers may not be shy about asking agents to cover any number of costs in a transaction, which may equal several thousand dollars. If an agent feels she can afford such requests and those costs don't violate any lender prohibitions, he or she may end up working for considerably less than the anticipated commission. This falls into the realm of negotiation skill and is the subject of other texts.

Ideally, agents will be skilled enough to avoid these pitfalls; otherwise, they may have to yield some expensive concessions until they do become that skilled.

It is important to understand that cost examples throughout this writing have intentionally been left open ended. It is impossible to be exact to the penny, and any number of these dollar amounts can change "without prior notice" in the marketplace. This is particularly true in the case of technology and material costs. There will always be someone who comes up with a widget that provides one more advantage than the one that already exists, and it may be purchased for a few dollars less.

Time and the purchaser's shopping acumen will also have their effect on costs. Learn to shop well, but learn to negotiate even better. The savings from both of these skills is priceless.

CHAPTER 8

▼

THE BALANCING ACT

The attempt to gain and maintain some sense of balance between the workweek and time away from work can be a challenge. When work activities become the priority and business gains momentum, it is easy for time to slip away, and agents often forget to schedule time away from work. Just the opposite happens when business is slow. Either period of activity can easily lure agents to go overboard in either direction.

When business is on the upswing, if balance is not maintained, personal relationships suffer. When business is ebbing, the work discipline is easily abandoned and work habits suffer. Both sides of the real estate business cycle must be kept in balance; otherwise the costs can be substantial in terms of lost money and lost personal relationships.

If there has been a lull in business and then suddenly a listing or buyer is obtained, it is very easy to overindulge by offering extreme service to the new seller or buyer to insure a payday in the near future. By overextending energy and attention on the new opportunity, other opportunities that become available may not be recognized, because too much attention is being focused on the first one.

New agents will have plenty of activities in which to participate and information to gather when they join their first broker. Learning inventory, contracts and forms used in the industry, and office procedures can keep the novice actively engaged for the first month in the new office. Until the broker is confident the new agent can effectively receive "up calls" and "walk-in" business, and has an acceptable knowledge of inventory, "covering the office floor" ("opportunity time") will not be offered to the new agent.

After the new agent can cover the floor and perhaps has a client, the schedule can get rather full very quickly. There are disclosures to be executed, inspections to be made, and competence to be exercised on the client throughout the transaction. These interactions do take a significant amount of time.

If ample time is not spent developing a good relationship with the client, the client will probably not be a repeat customer. A "repeat business base" should be the goal for all real estate agents. After the initial transaction is closed, there will need to be periodic contact with those clients in order to maintain them for future business. Not maintaining repeat business is very costly over the lifetime of the career.

Some believe the "shotgun approach" works best. This means that if an agent captures as many listings as possible, enough of them will sell to provide him with a good living. The agent need not worry about the ones that do not sell. Another agent will probably end up working those, but the easier money may be made by playing the "numbers game." This tactic may work well in densely populated areas, but if the community in which the agents lives and works is not large, the negative effect will eventually catch up with the agent, and his reputation can suffer over the long haul.

Some of the activities an agent must learn to fit into the work week are as follows: floor time, office meetings, appointments with clients/customers, broker tours, open houses, mailings to targeted areas and to past clients/customers, answering/returning phone calls, keeping abreast of inventory every day, previewing new listings before broker tour (if necessary), coordinating advertising, and attending seminars and association meetings.

Having the freedom to set personal appointments and run errands during the day can be easily fit into the Monday through Friday schedule. This is one of the perks of being an independent contractor. Because agents often work in the evenings and on weekends, when clients are most readily available, personal days off during the week should be scheduled as religiously as work-related commitments. If an agent is involved in a personal relationship or has a family, private time just for the agent alone is also very important.

A well-balanced schedule is necessary if marriages and personal relationships are to be maintained. Failing to reach a healthy balance between work and personal time can quickly become a recipe for disaster and can be quite costly for the agent's business or personal life—or both.

CHAPTER 9

▼

FINALLY, THE SILVER LINING!

No decent fairy tale ends without the characters living "happily ever after." Even though this explanation of the costs to the start-up real estate agent is no fairy tale, it would be unfair to end it without defending the rewards of becoming an agent. Yes, the cost of becoming an agent and maintaining a real estate career is expensive, but the reward can also be very lucrative. If not, there would be neither existing real estate agents nor future real estate agents.

Do not worry about real estate careers being outsourced. Realty agents perform indispensable services that are usually focused on the local level. No computer images can replace the firsthand knowledge and the knowledge of subtle details that an experienced realty agent provides to both buyer and seller. Skills that agents obtain throughout a real estate career are cumulative, and every transaction is different. Each one teaches an agent something more about the business.

Transactions are far too complex for the public to execute by itself without a great risk of being sued. Yes, real estate attorneys can be very valuable to a transaction, but their expertise is focused on matters that are different and often more restricted than those that real estate agents typically handle.

A standard disclosure for every agent should include, "Attorneys and CPA services are welcome and should be consulted immediately, if the client/customer feels they are needed or wants them involved during the transaction." Attorneys and CPAs may not need to be involved in most sales of property, but almost all property sales can benefit by a real estate agent's services.

The truth about financial rewards is that the annual income for most agents I have observed locally is less than $50,000 per year. However, I also know agents who earn $500,000 or more per year by specializing in high-end residential sales. Sales of commercial property and commercial and residential leasing can also be quite lucrative.

Agents acknowledge that, generally, 20 percent of the agents handle 80 percent of the business. An agent's success depends solely on that agent's ability and expertise. Another shop phrase is "An agent's raise is effective when the agent is." These tidbits of philosophy are not hard to understand. Almost anyone can be successful in a real estate career if she is of at least average intelligence and applies honest effort.

Careers, just like trains, must be built very carefully; otherwise both can quickly go off track. Many schools can help the novice prepare for a career in real estate. There are schools that offer just enough courses to obtain the license. Some offer more extensive courses and a stronger foundation, which will be really helpful to the beginning agent. Some colleges and universities offer a complete curriculum, and the graduate is licensed as a salesperson or broker upon receiving his diploma.

Obviously, money, time available, and depth of commitment determine which level of education the prospective agent chooses. The more education the new agent has, the easier and faster he will succeed.

So, for those of you who have not been discouraged or daunted by this writing and the magnitude of some of the basic financial and personal costs required to start and maintain a career as a Real Estate Agent—**welcome to the industry**.

2080292